THE

GREEN TEA

USER'S MANUAL

THE

GREEN TEA

USER'S MANUAL

Helen Gustafson

FOREWORD BY ALICE WATERS
ILLUSTRATIONS BY MEREDITH HAMILTON

CLARKSON POTTER / PUBLISHERS
NEW YORK

Published by Clarkson Potter/Publishers, New York, New York.
Member of the Crown Publishing Group.

Random House, Inc. New York, Toronto, London, Sydney, Auckland
www.randomhouse.com

CLARKSON N. POTTER is a trademark and POTTER and colophon
are registered trademarks of Random House, Inc.

The Tea Etymology Chart on page 18 is adapted from
All About Tea by William H. Ukers. Used by permission.

Printed in the United States of America

Design by Jan Derevjanik

Library of Congress Cataloging-in-Publication Data
Gustafson, Helen.
The green tea user's manual / Helen Gustafson.— 1st ed.
1. Cookery (Tea)   2. Green tea.   I. Title.
TX817.T3 G88 2001
641.6'372—dc21   2001021452

ISBN 0-609-60824-X

10 9 8 7 6 5 4 3 2 1

First Edition

ACKNOWLEDGMENTS

To my agent, Helen Pratt, for early inspiration and encouragement; to cousins Joan Gustafson and Barbara Hart for their enthusiasm; and to my husband, Gus, who every evening for forty years has said, "And tomorrow morning we'll have a nice cup of tea."

To my editor, Margot Schupf, for her incisive red pencil; to Meredith Hamilton for her delightful illustrations; and to Jan Derevjanik for her elegant design.

For professional help in tasting, sipping, reading, and providing, thanks to Tom Eck, Roy and Grace Fong, Russell Moore and Mario Daniele, Henry Patterson, Donna Lo Christy, Norwood Pratt, Todd Walton, Tom White, Joe and Joan Adams, and Elaine Ginger.

And for that special push: Maureen O'Shea-Shevshenko.

The rolling and roasting process
(for green tea) is called tatching, and when
the leaves rustle like paper, it is done.

JASON GOODWIN
from *A Time for Tea*

CONTENTS

Helen Gustafson is passionate about tea in ways that make perfect sense to a fellow perfectionist like myself. Over the years at Chez Panisse, I've trekked long distances to procure the finest lettuces, for example, or the seeds to grow them if the right lettuces couldn't be found. I've nurtured fantasies about the best approach to food and service, and tried to teach my coworkers to share my goals.

Helen's approach to tea and tea service is essentially the same: dogged, relentless, tireless, and enthusiastic. Ever since the day, years ago, when she suggested that the Darjeeling we were serving was inauthentic and inferior, we've depended upon Helen to educate us and keep us in line. My own tea knowledge was limited before Helen arrived in 1980. I'd learned to love tea in a bowl for breakfast as a student in France, and it was there that I first had fresh herbs brewed for a tisane after dinner. But under Helen's tutelage, I—along with my staff—discovered the varied pleasures of green tea, as well as the proper methods for brewing all kinds of other teas we'd never heard of or tried.

Simply put, Helen badgered us into taking the same care with tea that we did with everything else we served at Chez Panisse. She gave us the practical tools with which to do it, and her passion for tea was contagious. Along the way, a whole generation of diners learned with us.

We have Helen to thank for the beautiful Japanese iron teapots we use at the restaurant, and for the elegant, eclectic list of all-organic, pure-leaf teas we offer.

Helen's latest book gives practical advice to both the tea novice and the experienced tea drinker. It is filled with fascinating tea lore and Helen's irrepressible spirit, guiding you to make the right choices while demystifying the secrets of green tea. I hope you enjoy it as much as I have.

Alice Waters

What *Is* Green Tea?

Tea is nought but this:
First you heat the water,
Then you make the tea.
Then you drink it properly.
That is all you need to know.

RIKYU

*I*magine a largish budding rosebush, or better still, a waist-high camellia bush in early spring, its outer leaves small and shiny and freshly sprouted. If you wanted to make green tea from this bush, you would pluck the smallest, most delicate top leaves and throw them into a large, flat wicker basket, where they would be allowed to wither for a few hours. Then you'd "set" the leaves by dumping them into a big wok and lightly frying them, turning them again and again, drying them even further. Or you might put them in a big oven and dry them that way. The Chinese feel very strongly about the dangers of *damp* in the diet and in the body. You want to get the damp out of those leaves.

After baking or cooking them in a wok, you'd make big lumpy balls out of the leaves, and then you'd roll, twist, squeeze, and pummel them. When the leaves became soft and limp, and the smell and the look of them was just right, you'd be nearly finished. You'd give them one last blast of heat, then package them. Voilà: Green tea!

Making black tea is more complicated and takes longer—the leaves are exposed to the air until they blacken, just as a cut-up potato will turn black. Then they're pummeled and cut and rolled and made to wilt. The exposure to air (oxidizing) and cooking is repeated over and over, the process taking twenty-four hours or more.

But *all* tea, black, green, oolong, or white, comes from the same plant, *Camellia sinensus*. (*Sinensus* refers to China, where the plant originated.) All types of tea start out roughly the same—green leaves picked from a tea bush—it's how you process them that makes the difference.

The Joys of Green Tea

*A*nd green tea *is* different. It is "another cup of tea"—a phrase I've heard somewhere. It has its own aromas and delights. It's the music of flutes, not cellos, the feel of springtime, not cozy winter evenings. Green tea is subtler than black tea, but its effects are longer lasting. The smaller amounts of caffeine in greens are released very differently than in blacks. Caffeine from green tea follows an undulating wavelike pattern—a nearly steady, mild high. No big peaks, and no big plunges. I can, and do, work for hours sustained by this gentle push.

All greens, with only rare exceptions, need under-boiling water in the 160°–190°F. range. The easiest way to get to that range is to look at the water in an open, ordinary saucepan—four to five inches in diameter is ideal. Set aside your teakettle and take up the saucepan. Make tea the way the ancients did. The changing appearance of the water heating in the pan will tell you everything you need to know for a good cuppa green.

A story that went around Chez Panisse and brought a knowing smile to every face will illustrate this point. Natalie Waag, an old pal and mentor of Alice Waters, invited a group of foodies to her home in Provence to take cooking lessons. Every day the group would tour the open market and watch Natalie as she negotiated the choicest foodstuffs for the evening meal. After a long day, an exhausted man asked Natalie, "But how do I know when the cheese is right?"

"You look," she said. "You *look* at the cheese."

In just this way, you look at the water and know when it is *right*.

Lu Yu, the famous father of tea, described it in his book *Cha Ching,* written in A.D. 780.

When the water boils for the first time,
something akin to the eyes of a fish appear on the surface
and a faint hissing sound can be heard.

Then the gurgling brook develops
with a string of pearls round the edge.
This is the second boiling.

Then the turbulent waves appear: this is the third boiling.

Most greens taste best when the water is somewhere in the Fish Eyes (160°–180°F.) through String of Pearls (180°–190°F.) range. It's not hard to see these stages—in one short trial you'll know what to look for. In the next few pages, instructions will guide you. But the main idea is to let go of a Western dependence on shiny, bristling tools to do the job. Greens give us a chance to do things naturally, simply, intimately. If you want, you can avoid that whistling teakettle demanding to be poured this instant! The water for green tea can be poured within a minute or more of the correct moment and still make a perfectly delicious tea. No fancy thermometers or special equipment is needed. Ordinary, everyday utensils that are in your kitchen right now will do very nicely.

Someday you may want to purchase some small covered cups—called *guywans*—and graduate to the simplest, and in my opinion the best, way to make green teas. In the tea trade, this traditional covered cup is considered the best invention of the Chinese in two thousand years. But for now, all you need do is buy some green tea at the supermarket or from a health food store or mail-order house, get out the saucepan, heat up that water, and as Natalie Waag would say, "Look."

Black tea energizes me in the morning. And as I hover over my pot of Ceylon, inhaling that musky scent (called in the trade "fragrant breath of tea"), I remark on what a tonic it is. But lately I find a greater, longer-lasting tonic effect in green tea. I've learned how to make green tea properly so its impact can lift and sustain me through the day—millions of people in Japan and China can say the same. In Japan there are little street-corner stands that dispense green tea to passersby who keep their thermoses filled all day. They drink green tea continually, like water. And so should we.

I find that the craving for a sweet is banished if I drink a cup of green tea midafternoon; a slightly unsettled stomach is soothed, and in all cases, a steady satisfying calm slips into my body.

This is not so with black tea, the jump-start tea, I call it. That good old habit, taught to us by our mothers, of pouring water just at the moment of the boil has defeated many a would-be green tea drinker. The liquid emerges fried, scorched, and bitter. The drinker returns with a wry smile to stout black tea, or coffee with its quick caffeine high and the resulting sugar-craving low.

I hope this little book lets you into the world of green tea so you can drink it with pleasure all day long, and do what the doctor ordered—and Mother Nature, too.

Years ago, a leading tea man said to me in his heavy European accent, "Black tea I know; this is physics. Green tea I don't know; this is chemistry." Then, waving his big hands palms out, he thrust "chemistry" away off—toward China. Though living on the Pacific Rim, he was pushing the Far East farther away, knowing in the back of his mind that all it had to bring us was on the way.

Tea Etymology Chart

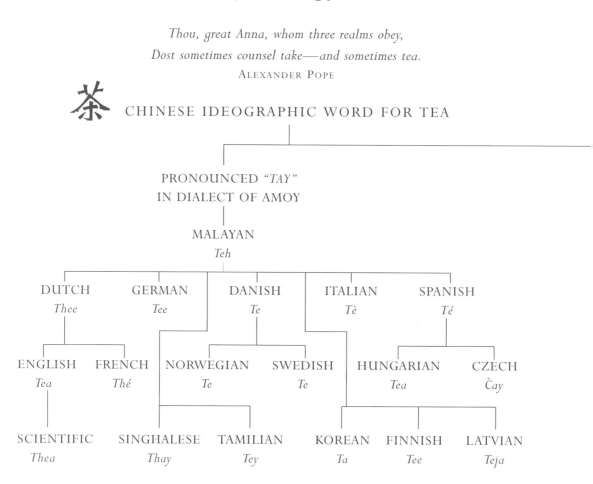

茶 CHINESE IDEOGRAPHIC WORD FOR TEA

PRONOUNCED *"TAY"*
IN DIALECT OF AMOY

MALAYAN
Teh

DUTCH	GERMAN	DANISH	ITALIAN	SPANISH
Thee	*Tee*	*Te*	*Tè*	*Té*

ENGLISH	FRENCH	NORWEGIAN	SWEDISH	HUNGARIAN	CZECH
Tea	*Thé*	*Te*	*Te*	*Tea*	*Čay*

SCIENTIFIC	SINGHALESE	TAMILIAN	KOREAN	FINNISH	LATVIAN
Thea	*Thay*	*Tey*	*Ta*	*Tee*	*Teja*

$\mathcal{T}$he famous couplet by Alexander Pope refers to England's lonely Queen Anne (1665–1714), and its rhyme depends on the word *tea* being pronounced *tay*. This makes sense when you understand the origin of the word and how it came to be part of the English language.

The chart below not only gives us the different words for tea around the world, but also shows the routes tea took as it spread across the globe. You will note that the original Chinese words *Tay* and *Ch'a* remain relatively unaltered regardless of which culture they collide with, suggesting that the substance is perfectly named.

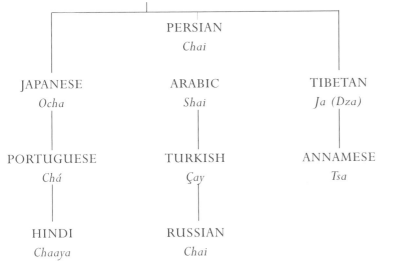

PRONOUNCED "CH'A"
IN PURE CANTONESE

PERSIAN
Chai

JAPANESE
Ocha

ARABIC
Shai

TIBETAN
Ja (Dza)

PORTUGUESE
Chá

TURKISH
Çay

ANNAMESE
Tsa

HINDI
Chaaya

RUSSIAN
Chai

Health Benefits of Green Tea*

*One study found that the concentration of polyphenols
in one cup of tea was two to three times greater
than that needed to kill some bacteria.*

NADINE TAYLOR FROM
GREEN TEA: THE NATURAL SECRET FOR A HEALTHIER LIFE

You've no doubt heard green tea is very good for you. The leaves are so green and fresh, like a vegetable—some really fresh ones from Japan are bright green—they even *look* healthy. The many health benefits of green tea appear to have an edge over those of black tea at the time of this writing, though studies over the past few years have offered praise for both. Here are some of the key benefits that may result from regular consumption of green tea.

Green tea helps prevent normal cells from turning cancerous, slows the formation and growth of tumors, and lessens damage from free radicals that can cause cancer, heart disease, diabetes, and aging. It also clearly enhances immune system function, helps control cholesterol, keeps blood sugar at moderate levels, and combats viruses and deadly food-borne bacteria. Furthermore, green tea promotes the growth of beneficial bacteria in the intestines and encourages bowel regularity.

---

*Sources of health benefits information: Andrew Weil's *Self Healing* newsletter, Lester Mitscher and Victoria Dolby's *The Green Tea Book,* Nadine Taylor's *Green Tea,* the National Institute of Public and Environmental Protection of the Netherlands, the University of Wisconsin Health Department, the University of Michigan Health Department, the *Harvard Health Newsletter,* the *Tufts University Health Newsletter,* and the report from the Tea Quality and Human Health Symposium, Hangzhou, China.

Green tea also produces a mild stimulating effect without causing insomnia or nervousness, kills bacteria in the mouth that cause cavities and bad breath, and may even slow the aging process by enhancing the body's fluid balance and reducing stress. Finally, green tea is widely used as a natural preservative in food and cosmetics.

All over Cathay [China] they made use of another plant called Chai Catai [tea of China]. They take of that herb, whether dry or fresh, and boil it well in water. One or two cups of this decoction taken on an empty stomach removes fever, headache, stomach ache, pain in the sides or in the joint. It is so highly valued and esteemed that everyone going on a journey takes it with him, and those people would gladly give a sack of rhubarb for one ounce of Chai Catai.

RAMUSIO, A.D. 1559

About Caffeine in Tea

There is an enormous amount of information about caffeine out there today, much of it contradictory. The widely held notion that green tea has less caffeine than black tea is true, but not because of the length of time the tea leaves have been "fermented" (actually oxidized—exposed to air).

Caffeine content depends largely on the size and type of the tea leaf used—the larger the leaf, the less caffeine. In this book, readers are urged to drink large-leaf teas that contain less caffeine than other green teas. Also, since several steepings are possible with each serving of the larger leaf teas—and the caffeine content is less with each steeping—your caffeine intake will be much lower with the better teas recommended in this book.

Caffeine Facts You Might Want to Know

*T*here are several factors that determine the amount of caffeine in your tea. The leaf-to-water ratio is a major determinant in the caffeine content of your tea. That is, the less leaf you use, the less caffeine possible. The shape and size of your brewing vessel will also influence caffeine content, because the larger the area of circulation, the more caffeine will be drawn from the leaves.

Factors influencing the effects caffeine will have on you are your own particular sensitivity to caffeine in relation to the time of day, and the emptiness or fullness of your stomach. If you have kidney problems, an irregular heartbeat, or high blood pressure, be careful of caffeine.

Leaves of tea plants grown under shade will develop more caffeine in them than those grown in the open. The highest caffeine levels are found in the top two leaves and a bud, otherwise known as the Imperial Pluck, whereas tea leaves picked from the lower parts of the bush, such as Bancha, have much less caffeine than those picked from the higher parts. Gen Mai Cha, which is half brown rice, will have less caffeine than one that's all tea.

Teas that are processed by high firing (quickly in a hot wok) have less caffeine than those processed more slowly. Dragon Well and Bi Luo Chun are high-fired in woks. And in general, Chinese teas have less caffeine than Indian teas.

How to Decaffeinate Your Tea at Home

This is a process that works only for fine teas; otherwise the resulting tea will have very little flavor. Unfortunately, the decaffeinating process also removes most of the beneficial antioxidants in tea.

1. Brew your green tea for thirty seconds.
2. Pour off the liquid and set aside to use for watering your houseplants.
3. Start all over again with the used leaves, and brew according to your taste.

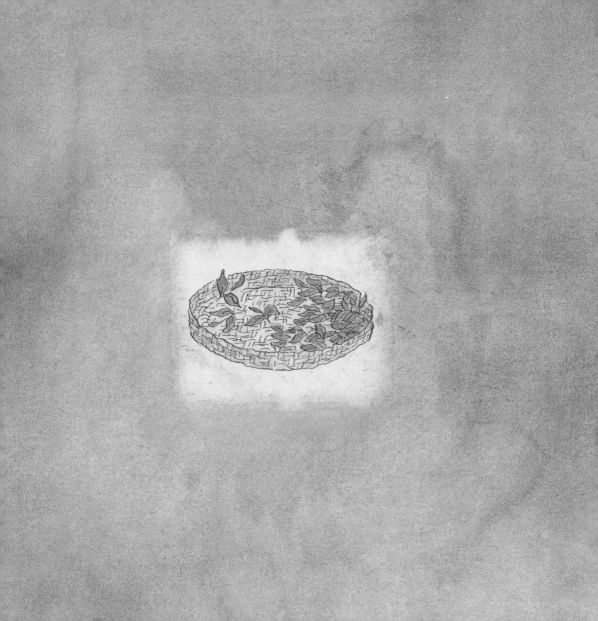

THE WATER FOR TEA

How to Be Sure Your Water Is Good Enough

Meanwhile let us have a sip of tea.
The afternoon glow is brightening the bamboos,
the fountains are bubbling with delight,
the soughing of the pines is heard in our kettle.
Let us dream of evanescence, and linger in the
beautiful foolishness of things.

KAKUZO OKAKURA

*W*ater for good tea is best when it is *entirely* free of chlorine, low in alkalinity, and soft (not cloudy and scummy), with a clean, clear, crisp taste. Mountain spring water is the first choice of Chinese connoisseurs.

How to Get Good Water

1. Use a Brita or Everpure filter. These filters are inexpensive and reduce chlorine and mineral content (TDS—total dissolved solids).

2. Buy bottled, noncarbonated springwater (in bottles and jugs) and check the content label. The best waters for green teas will be marked with a pH of 7 and a TDS of 40 to 50.

3. Install a home water-filtering system. This will reduce the minerals, chlorine, mold, and alkalinity in your water. It is more expensive but very efficient. Be sure to get a system with a carbon *block,* rather than one with carbon *flakes.* The block will need replacement about once every six months, or even once a year, depending on use.

Classic Temperatures for Brewing Tea

Water temperature is crucial to the taste of your tea. By choice or accident you will find yourself experimenting with a range of temperatures for brewing your favorite teas. To avoid disappointment (and bitterness) I highly recommend you begin with the suggested temperatures. Also, do not use aluminum, tin, or cast-iron saucepans, which may impart an unpleasant metallic taste to your tea.

There are some eminent Chinese scholars who believe there are five identifiable stages in the boiling of water. But to keep things simple, I've included only the classic three.

Fish Eyes (160°–180°F.)

Pin-size (⅛-inch-diameter) bubbles reminiscent of the eyes of a fish begin to rise to the surface, and a faint hissing sound can be heard. Extremely delicate green teas brew well at the lower end of this temperature spectrum.

String of Pearls (180°–190°F.)

When bubbles break the surface and/or begin to cling to the sides of the pan, they are called String of Pearls. Most common (everyday) green teas and many finer teas do very well at this temperature.

Turbulent Waters (190°–210°F.)

Large bubbles (⅓-inch diameter) break the surface. They will appear rather quickly after the String of Pearls. In the Western world we call this a rolling boil. Very few green teas require this temperature.

I have found that the finer green teas do very well when made at the moment that the bubbles first begin to gather on the bottom of the saucepan. Lu Yu, in his classic treatise on tea, devotes quite a few paragraphs to managing the second stage of boiling, called String of Pearls (180°–190°F.). He goes on to fiddle around with that particular temperature, declaring it just right for most green teas.

This tea bears three waters well.

FROM AN EARLY ADVERTISEMENT FOR GREEN TEA

Another Way of Looking at Hot Water

If you have allowed the water to reach the Turbulent Waters stage (boiling), and it is not the temperature you want, one remedy is to lift the saucepan to eye level (not in front of a window) and observe the steam as it rises. If the entire column of steam is rising straight up, it is still very close to a full boil. When the steam starts to drift (becomes lazy), the temperature is low enough to use for most green teas. Warning: Beware of drafts!

The Standard Mug Method

A good way to make any green tea for those without a teapot

YOU WILL NEED:

Two large mugs

A strainer—common handheld type

A timer

A small saucepan

A tin of loose green tea

1. Measure 2 heaping teaspoons of dry leaf into one of the mugs.

2. Heat 2 to 3 cups of cold, filtered water in the saucepan.

3. Bring water to the temperature recommended in the recipe for that specific tea.

4. Pour water into the mug.

5. Set the timer for approximately 2 minutes.

6. When the timer sounds, place the strainer over the other mug.

7. Pour the contents of the first mug into the second.

8. Remove the strainer, wait a minute or so, and enjoy your tea.

NOTE: IF IN DOUBT WHEN BREWING *ANY* GREEN TEA, ALWAYS USE A LOWER WATER TEMPERATURE.

USER'S TIP: FOR THE STANDARD MUG METHOD YOU MIGHT WANT TO USE A *ZHONG*, A FAIRLY NEW INVENTION—A STANDARD COFFEE MUG WITH A LID. IF YOU DO USE A *ZHONG*, WHEN YOU REMOVE THE STRAINER (IN STEP 8 ABOVE), PLACE THE LID ON THE MUG TO ENHANCE THE BREWING PROCESS.

USER'S TIP: IT IS ALWAYS BEST TO WAIT AT LEAST ONE MINUTE BEFORE DRINKING THE TEA TO ALLOW THE FLAVOR TO DEVELOP A BIT MORE IN THE CUP.

The Standard Pot Method

For a three- to four-cup teapot

YOU WILL NEED:

A teapot

An infusion basket

A small saucepan

A timer

A tin of loose green tea

1. Measure 3 to 4 teaspoons of dry leaf into an infusion basket and place into the teapot.

2. Start heating 3 to 4 cups of cold, filtered water in the saucepan.

3. Bring water to the temperature recommended in the recipe for that specific tea.

4. Pour water into the teapot.

5. Set the timer for approximately 2 minutes.

6. When the timer sounds, remove the infusion basket.

7. Pour the tea into your favorite cup.

NOTE: IF IN DOUBT WHEN BREWING *ANY* GREEN TEA, ALWAYS USE A LOWER WATER TEMPERATURE.

USER'S TIP: IF YOU ARE USING A LARGE TEAPOT (6 TO 8 CUPS OR MORE), REMEMBER THIS RATIO: 1 TEASPOON DRY LEAF PER CUP OF WATER.

The Standard Guywan Method
(Also known as Chung)

The guywan (Chinese covered cup) can be used for all green teas, and when all is said and done, I find using a guywan is the best way to control the strength and temperature of my tea so I can make it exactly as I like it. We are all used to the English-style teapot—and green teas can be made that way—but in time, most tea enthusiasts turn to the Chinese covered cup.

There is something so intimate about bringing the water to the proper temperature, standing by it at the stove, then pouring it carefully down the side of the guywan to the waiting leaves. The cup is warm in your hand, and the sound of the lid settling into place as you carry it across the room is like waves reaching shore under a pier—a summertime watery slap-slap that never fails to enchant.

YOU WILL NEED:

A guywan

A small saucepan

A tin of high-quality loose green tea

THE POOR MAN'S GUYWAN

A teacup (preferably white inside)

A soupspoon (for stirring the leaves)

A saucer to place over the teacup (to keep your tea warm)

1. Cover the bottom of the *guywan* with a layer of dry leaf.
2. Start heating 2 to 3 cups of cold, filtered water in the saucepan.
3. Bring water to Fish Eyes (160° to 180°F.) stage.
4. Pour water into the *guywan,* and cover.
5. Lift the lid and stroke the water to stir the leaves for a moment.
6. Take a peek to see if the leaves have settled to the bottom.
7. Use the lid as a strainer, letting only the liquor through as you sip.

BREWING TIP: AFTER THE FIRST CUP, POUR AGAIN WITH THE RESERVED OR SLIGHTLY REHEATED WATER. A HIGH-QUALITY TEA CAN USUALLY BE REPLENISHED TWO OR THREE TIMES.

The Standard Kettle Method

For the impatient, the pressed-for-time, and my friend Todd Watton,
who taught me this method.
This technique can be useful and speedy, and allows you to use your old, familiar teakettle
to boil your water. This method has even been adopted by some fine restaurants.

For a 3- to 4-Cup Teapot

1. For most green teas, measure 3 teaspoons of dry leaf in the infusion basket and measure it in the teapot.

2. Cover the tea leaves with about ½ cup of cold water.

3. Allow the water in your kettle to come to a boil.

4. Pour the hot water into the pot, where it will cool down as it marries with the cold water to produce the appropriate temperature.

5. Wait about 2 minutes and remove the infusion basket.

For the Guywan

1. Place 1 heaping teaspoon of dry leaf into the cup.

2. Add enough cold water to just cover the leaves.

3. Allow the water in your kettle to come to a boil.

4. Pour the hot water into the cup, where it will cool down as it marries with the cold water to produce the appropriate temperature.

5. Stir the tea with the lid, dipping deep into the cup.

6. Wait about 2 minutes and drink the tea.

BUYING A TEAPOT

*W*hen buying a teapot, I've often wondered why the British ones from Staffordshire are always recommended: "The best, you know." After a bit of research, the simple answer comes: most Staffordshire clays are made into porcelain (also called china). The product is dense, with few or no impurities, and it keeps the tea warmer for a longer time than teapots made of earthenware, which has more impurities—more airholes. Both types of pots are glazed with brilliant colors, so it's hard to tell them apart. But for green teas that are drunk at 160° to 180°F., instead of the hallowed 212°F. for black teas, either pot is acceptable. Part of black tea's bracing hit is its high heat. Not so with green tea, where the flavor is extracted best at a lower temperature.

Most porcelain pots, if they have a nice smooth surface on the inside (so important for thorough and easy cleaning), are about the same. And although it's fun to buy a Brown Betty from Staffordshire and uphold British tradition, it's not necessary for your green tea adventure. Staffordshire pots have a loyal following, but any well-made porcelain pot will do very nicely. And if you have a choice, I'd recommend buying porcelain.

How to choose, how to tell the difference between porcelain and earthenware? When you become familiar with the teapots as you handle them, you'll soon get a feel for the denseness, and notice the balanced heft, of a

Tetsubin

Rice pattern

Brown Betty

Lusterware

porcelain pot. The earthenware ones will not feel as heavy, be as expensive, or seem as "put together" as the porcelain—but they can serve you well. Don't worry about the terms *pottery, stoneware, soft paste, hard paste, creamware,* and so on. Rely on your senses to tell you which is the best pot for you. If you are taken with a whimsical earthenware beauty, there is no harm in buying it. Just remember: it will not clean as easily, and it is more likely to break than the porcelain ones.

For either type of pot:

- Look at the spout before you buy. Is it at the top of the pot? It should be, or you won't be able to completely fill the pot.

- The lid should fit snugly into place to retain heat and to keep you from having to hold it as you pour.

- The handle should be big enough for your fingers, or anyone else's fingers (bigger or smaller), to fit in an easy and balanced fashion.

- The whole pot should feel balanced. And make sure it won't topple over when nudged or empty.

- Look at the top opening. Is it big enough for an infusion basket or tea ball to fit into? Is it big enough to admit a scrub brush for internal cleaning?

- Is the inside smooth so it can be easily cleaned?

- Will you be comfortable looking at it daily? Some whimsical pots are fun at first, but will their appeal last a lifetime?

The stylish and popular *tetsubin* cast-iron Japanese pots are wonderful and they never break. They also keep the tea warm for a long time and do not require a tea cozy, making them a good choice for restaurants. Look at the inside of the *tetsubin* pot—the best ones have a shiny, ceramic glaze that will prevent rust. Some will have just a soft sheen—these have been seasoned. If you have that type, or buy one, be sure to dry it thoroughly after each use. Use a tea towel or invert the pot over a low flame for a minute or two.

Glass pots are fine for green teas and herbal infusions, often called by the French name, *tisanes*. Glass allows you to watch the agony of the leaves as they swirl and settle to the bottom of the pot. True, glass does not retain heat as well as ceramic or metal pots, but this is not particularly important with green teas.

In the China- or Japantowns of large cities in the United States you will sometimes find earthenware terra-cotta pots. These are traditional for oolong teas. They should only be rinsed out and never be washed with soap or detergent. The residue of the tea liquor over many pourings will imbue the lining with a silken residue. After some years, no tea leaves are needed to make the tea—only hot water is required. These pots will do for green tea, but if so used, do not use them to brew any other type of tea.

A Note on Infusion Baskets

The "rule" on infusion baskets (or strainers) is quite simple: to be successful they should nearly fill the entire space inside the teapot. There are many types available: tea socks (cotton fabric), paper filters (disposable envelopes), wire-mesh balls, polyester and wire-mesh baskets, cylindrical mesh inserts, ceramic inserts, and the simple handheld bamboo basket, so popular in the 1970s for herbal teas.

All types can be used with great success so long as the infusion vehicle is in correct proportion to the vessel being used: pot, mug, or cup. The basket should allow enough room for the leaves to unfurl and swirl about, without which really tasty tea cannot come into being. This means that the stylish "press pot" with the narrow, vertical plunger is *not* a good choice.

When buying an infusion device, keep in mind the size of the top opening of the teapot—the wider the better. Many modern pots have a spacious opening, but older models do not. If you have such an old, favorite pot, brew the tea without an infusion basket, then transfer the tea into a second pot. This will yield a better-tasting tea than you will get with an inadequate infusion basket.

Do *not* use the popular tea nut, or egg—a small, double-sided spoon, perforated with tiny holes. This device, so minuscule and so inadequate (and one of my personal pet peeves), makes a dreary cup of tea.

Gen Mai Cha will always hold a place of special affection for me, since it is connected with a major breakthrough in my relationship to tea, both as tea buyer for Chez Panisse, and as a student of the art of tea.

Big shifts in how a restaurant operates can happen unexpectedly—and in a single telling moment. One evening we might run out of a key ingredient to a popular dish, substitute something unusual in its place, name the new creation for the farm from which it came, and find that we've created a taste sensation that might stay on the menu for years and years.

I was involved in just such a moment in the mid-1980s when I was still fairly new to my role as tea buyer. One of my tea sources was Roy Fong of the Imperial Tea Court in San Francisco. When I first got to know him, he was one of many tea sources for the restaurant—just Roy, a calmly resourceful man with an encyclopedic knowledge of tea. Only later did I learn that he was the only practicing tea master in the Western Hemisphere.

I ordered a Gen Mai Cha from him, and when it arrived, I found it so subtle, so clean and clear, that I barely recognized it as a Gen Mai Cha. And though I loved it, I sent it back to Roy and urged him to come down to a more popular taste, more robust and toasty. "You can bring out this subtle one later," I suggested, "when the public is more educated, but we must appeal to their taste level now."

So Roy blended a new Gen Mai Cha, making sure the green leaves and the brown rice were roasted in concert with one another, making sure the leaf didn't overpower the puffed rice kernels, and taking care that the quantities of each were perfectly proportioned—a delicate balance.

This new Gen Mai Cha immediately became one of our best-selling teas, and later Roy confessed that this particular blend had become a favorite of every Japanese restaurant in San Francisco, and that it had "paid the rent" during an early lean time in his business.

I was delighted not only to have been of help, but to realize I now had a partner in producing exquisite teas that were finely honed to my own particular specifications—a unique luxury. Roy and I have continued to work hand in hand this way, and the Imperial Tea Court remains the principal supplier of Chez Panisse tea.

GEN MAI CHA

Brown Rice Tea

$\mathcal{G}$en Mai Cha is a popular, inexpensive, everyday drink in Japan. Kids drink it after school much the way that American kids will knock down a chocolate milk or cocoa. Frugal housewives probably invented this tea by stretching the precious tea with popped brown rice (or corn or barley) to make it go further.

A good Gen Mai Cha has a nice balance of properly popped rice and the green tea leaf roasted "just enough." It's toasty and unthreatening and a good choice for starting your green tea adventure. It's hard to make a bad cup of this tea. It can be made in a pot, too, but on the next page you'll find a simple way to get acquainted with this earthy drink that harmonizes the taste of toasted grain with the flavor of tea.

Brewing Gen Mai Cha

(See The Standard Mug Method on page 29.)

1. Bring the water to Turbulent Waters stage (190°–210°F., unusually hot for a green tea, but necessary to bring out the flavor of the brown rice).

2. Measure 3 heaping teaspoons of Gen Mai Cha into a mug.

3. When the water is turbulent, pour water into the mug.

4. Set the timer for 2 minutes.

5. When the timer sounds, place a strainer over another mug and pour the contents of the first mug into the second.

6. Remove the strainer and wait a minute or so. The tea is ready.

Replacing a Favorite

When I first began to order teas for Chez Panisse in 1982, fruit-flavored black tea had been popular and stylish in California for about a decade. Patrons and staff used to query me about why we didn't serve one. My reason was simple. Although I knew perfectly well that Earl Grey and jasmine were well established, the newer teas flavored with tropical fruits struck me as unworthy. I favored pure leaf teas and still do.

Then a friend called to say she had found a good peach tea in Paris, better than the raspberry one that was all the rage there that season. I recalled that peach was a term often used in descriptions of fine Darjeelings, and reasoned that the peach flavor might marry very well with any good black tea. We needed a new iced tea, and when I learned that this peach tea came from the same German firm that made the fruit juice reductions used by the fabulous gelato makers of Italy, I was sold and peach tea was on.

What the customers didn't inhale that day, the staff did, and there was none left by five o'clock. That peach tea became a menu staple for nearly twenty years. People would approach me on the street, winter and summer, and declare, "What brings me to Chez Panisse is that peach tea!" The balance of sweetness to tartness was just right, and the caffeine gave that much desired little lift. It went well with bread and butter as well as with desserts and main dishes.

When Alice announced we would serve only organic foods by 2000, I began my search for a substitute for the peach tea. Waiters and bussers and everyone from cooks to dishwashers used the peach tea as a favorite pick-me-up. Soon the anguished pleas came to me: "Do we really have to give it up? I can't stand working without it." Procuring, testing, and installing a tea that "suits" is usually a protracted and tortuous task, with false leads and dead ends. The peach tea was a maverick success story, and I despaired of finding a worthy replacement.

And then one warm fall evening, my mentor and pal, Norwood Pratt, phoned to say he was coming by to drop off some teas. Bulky, lumpy bags filled with smaller packets of tea often flow between the members of our little tea family. We all get free samples from tea brokers hoping to sell. We taste them and share what's left over from this near-constant supply of two- to eight-ounce little packets. We call each other to gossip and compare, indulging in the jargon that develops in all such subcultures. "I thought it was winey with such a long finish." "Oh, I thought it was rather flat and biscuity."

"Here's this Citron Green," said Norwood. "Mike Harney has it. Organic. Says it's madly popular in the South."

A half hour later he was gone. I brewed it immediately and found my cup of Citron Green vigorous and assertive and "nice" but not a tea to grab my attention. Then I remembered that Southerners do love iced tea, and I thought this tea would be terrific iced. Well, but maybe a lit- tle too sweet—it wouldn't suit most foods. So I let it go. But the memory of its intriguing, slightly bitter bite at the finish haunted me. Suddenly my fist came down on the table. This would be the iced tea to replace the wildly pop- ular black peach blend. For months I had been going through cup after cup of liquids that seemed to be brewed from straw. Citron Green was my answer.

The decision had been as quick and sure as with the peach tea—an excellent harbinger for success. But it was a harrowing route from my fist on the table to the large latte glasses of that pale and lovely green liquid on the tables of Chez Panisse. The mixture was made up of green tea—a mix of Sencha, ginkgo (good for the brain and quite fashionable), and citronella (lemongrass, a natural sweetener). It was nearly right, but perhaps it could be improved. I called Mike Harney and asked him to give us an exclusive on this privately blended Citron Green, with less ginkgo and less citronella. In return, I would use his company's name on the menu.

A few weeks later, the tea arrived and it was perfect. All I had to do now was figure out the right proportions to make five gallons a day, and I would be set. After a week of nearly con- stant experimentation, the tea made its well- received public debut. Emblematic of the public reaction to the tea was a smiling customer who gushed, "Do you do the tea here? Well, this new iced tea is even better than the peach. So refreshing, so surprising." I sauntered proudly back to the bar and had a large glass myself.

With the new Citron Green iced tea safely on the menu, I realized that we had a half-chest of peach tea left. I began to feel sorry for the new crop of peach tea—deprived persons and arranged to sell it to the man- ager of a delicatessen down the street, a former Chez Panisse cook. I fantasized the actual removal: a small, cheerful throng of stalwarts carrying a PEACH TEA FOREVER banner, the press hovering about, the flashing cameras, the opening of the delicatessen door, heaving the heavy chest through to waiting hands and the relieved sighs of the waiting patrons. Of course, I just took it down on a dolly with a sturdy helper, gave some instructions, and left. The customers did look grateful, though.

Every good tea director tries to keep a few old favorites (Earl Grey, English Breakfast) on hand at the restaurant but at the same time stretch the customer's palate by introducing new and sometimes subtle teas. At Chez Panisse, introducing new ways of eating has always been the underlying principle.

To justify the purchase of a new product, and an expensive one, to the supervising chef or manager, a cook or wine/coffee/tea buyer has only to say, "Well, it's the best," and the new offering will have a fair chance of capturing the audience. The idea of excellence—I love that.

GUNPOWDER

(Also called Pearl Tea or Zhucha)

$\mathcal{G}$unpowder is to green tea what Ivory is to soap—it's been around forever, it's everywhere, and because of this it is often the first kind of green tea urged on the curious newcomer. Gunpowder was one of the first loose-leaf green teas widely sold in the United States and one of the first green teas available from mail-order houses. The name is intriguing, promising a powerful, even explosive lift. But above all, as tea merchants well know, those little, tightly rolled, gray-green pellets make Gunpowder a keeper with a long shelf life.

Unfortunately, Gunpowder can be an extremely troublesome tea. It is made with a blend of old and new leaves, and if the mixture is a poor one, or if in brewing the leaves are oversteeped, no tea can turn more bitter so quickly. Countless prospective green tea drinkers have been turned off to green tea *entirely* by starting with an inferior Gunpowder.

When my cousin dutifully sipped her first Gunpowder, she turned to me in all innocence and said, "Does it have black tea in it?" I knew I had some explaining to do. Indeed, it does have that sharp, near-bitter edge that black tea can have, and it's very filling, much like many black teas, which is another reason why starting your adventure into green tea with Gunpowder is like learning to swim by jumping off the high diving board before you know how to dog-paddle.

Gunpowder—also known in the early days as Imperial—comes in various grades, and if you're going to try it, buy the highest grade you can afford.

Brewing Gunpowder

(See The Standard Mug Method on page 29.)

1. Measure 2 teaspoons of dry leaf into a strainer. Place in a mug.

2. Start heating 2 to 3 cups of cold, filtered water in a saucepan.

3. When Fish Eyes (160°–180°F.) break the surface, pour the water over the leaves.

4. Set the timer for 2 minutes. When the timer sounds, remove the strainer and pour the tea into another mug.

5. Set the timer for 1 more minute.

6. When timer sounds, the tea is ready to drink.

NOTE: YOU MAY ALSO USE THE STANDARD POT METHOD ON PAGE 30 OR THE STANDARD GUYWAN METHOD ON PAGE 32

BUYER'S TIP: START WITH A HIGH-GRADE GUNPOWDER. IF THE TEA IS PURCHASED FROM A REPUTABLE MAIL-ORDER HOUSE (PAGE 107), PRICE IS DEFINITELY AN INDICATOR OF QUALITY. FORTUNATELY, EVEN THE HIGHEST GRADE OF GUNPOWDER IS NOT TOO EXPENSIVE.

⟨leaf ornament⟩

*I*n the early days of the tea trade, the Chinese were forbidden by their emperor to speak to the foreign devils—the British—who were trading opium for tea. And so, legend has it, rather than go to all the trouble, and possibly danger, of learning the Chinese name for the little round balls of green tea, the British named it what it looked like to them—Gunpowder.

⟨leaf ornament⟩

Tea is a work of art and needs a master hand to bring out its noblest qualities.

KAKUZO OKAKURA

*T*ea authority James Norwood Pratt once declared with his distinguished profile held high that Gunpowder, so difficult to brew, so ubiquitous, such an impediment to bringing the real joys of green tea to the greater public, should be banned from entry into the United States.

SIMPLE GREENS

*A*fter the comforting toastiness of Gen Mai Cha, next on the green tea journey might be a simple green, the *vin ordinaire* of the green tea world. In tea jargon this kind of tea is called an "everyday drink." Though simple greens will play a valuable role in your tea world, we won't linger long with them. There are too many wonderful—truly "full of wonder"—teas that will light up your life and lighten your load as well.

These simple greens go by many names, including Yunnan Green, China Green, Chunmee, Soumee, Hyson, Young Hyson, and Eshan Pekoe. One key to identifying them is that they are all relatively inexpensive. The best one I ever had was a Japanese variety bought at the huge Tokyo fish market. It came in a green-speckled package stamped with a mystifyingly simple Japanese character that translated roughly as "Fresh," or "New." And sometimes the packets of simple green teas found in health food stores will state with blunt clarity "GREEN." If it's inexpensive, try it.

Most important, avoid the common introductory offer found in many mail-order catalogs: a sweetened green tea. This is the old sugarcoated-pill ruse. Don't fall for it. Properly brewed green tea, all by itself, has a natural sweetness that precludes the need for any artificial additions. Some green teas are sweetened naturally with citronella or mint. They can be tasty—but a pure green tea is the best way to start tasting green teas. You can drink pure leaf green tea all day long without feeling full—a wonderful health-enhancing habit.

COMMON EXPRESSIONS DERIVED FROM TEA

A nice old cup of tea (British): A sweet person.

Chali (Chinese): A tea gift given to a woman upon her engagement.

He has no tea in him (Japanese): Said of a person with little life in him.

Hock nit kein Chainik (Yiddish): Literally means, "Don't bang a teakettle." Don't make such a big fuss. Don't bother me.

Let the tea steep (German): Forget about it.

Na chai (Russian): Literally, "For the tea." The tip one leaves in a restaurant.

Not for all the tea in China: Not at any price.

Not my cup of tea: It isn't anything I like.

Teetotal: To abstain from intoxicating drinks.

Tempest in a teapot: Much ado about nothing.

That's another cup of tea (British): Another angle on a story.

What's that got to do with the price of tea?: Why is that important?

Tea Lore

Yunnan Green

*O*nce you've had a tasty Yunnan Green, you'll recognize the taste no matter what the label reads. Perhaps it is so satisfying because the world's original tea plants come from Yunnan province, high in the center of southern China. The greatest pleasure of these simple greens often comes not in the mouth, but afterward in the overall good feeling in the body. It is certainly one of those marvelous mysteries of the tea-drinking life, but when I drink a simple Yunnan Green, I often feel I have a gentle beaming, pale green sun radiating goodness and warmth right there in the middle of my solar plexus long after I've consumed a small pot of it. My favorite of all the simple greens is Yunnan Green. Here's the recipe:

Brewing Yunnan Green

(See The Standard Pot Method on page 30.)

The key to brewing Yunnan and other simple greens is to make certain the water is in the String of Pearls temperature range (approximately 165°–185°F.). Brew for two minutes only and wait at least one minute after the liquor (liquid) has been in the cup before drinking. After drinking the first cup, the one-minute wait is not needed. The tea will develop a bit more—get stronger—but it will not get bitter.

1. Measure 3 to 4 teaspoons of dry leaf into an infusion basket and place in a pot.

2. Start heating 3 to 4 cups of cold, filtered water in a saucepan.

3. When Fish Eyes (160°–180°F.) start to break the surface and/or the tiny String of Pearls rim the edge of the pan, pour the water over the leaves.

4. Set the timer for 2 minutes. When the timer sounds, remove the infusion basket and pour the tea into a cup.

5. Set the timer for 1 more minute.

6. When the timer sounds, begin to drink.

NOTE: You may also use The Standard Mug Method on page 29 or The Standard *Guywan* Method on page 32.

USER'S TIP: Simple green teas, possessing little complexity, often require more care in the brewing than expensive green tea—just as a cheap cotton shirt requires a pressing every time it is worn to look good, while a heavy silk shirt can be worn time after time and still be presentable. The more complex, more mouth-filling teas, always more expensive than the simple greens, are called the "forgiving teas." They can be almost carelessly brewed. Too little leaf, too short or too long a steeping time? No matter. They will still taste very, very good.

BUYER'S TIP: With inexpensive simple greens, it's always best to drink them up within a few days or weeks of purchase—the fresher the better.

BUYER'S TIP: The fresh, elusive Japanese Green can sometimes be snagged in Japantowns in large cities. It usually has almost no appellation at all, just the assurance from the shopkeeper that it *is* fresh. It might be! Try it. In Japan, when these new green teas are two weeks old, you will see them in department stores being sold at half price because they are considered *so* old.

ROASTED TEAS

Bancha ～ *Hojicha* ～ *Kukicha*
(Bahn-cha) *(Ho-jee-cha)* *(Kook-key-cha)*

*T*hese chippy-choppy names skip across the page like chubby little kittens. But these are not young teas. These Japanese mainstays are made from the lowest leaves and/or twigs of the tea bush—a kind of cleanup at the end of the harvest.

Bancha means "last tea," Hojicha means "roasted tea," and Kukicha means "twig tea." *Cha* is the universal word for tea. Inexpensive, yet wonderfully satisfying when brewed correctly, these teas have legions of avid fans. They are not complex teas, but they "present"—reveal their taste— all at once in the mouth, so you know instantly what they have to offer. By contrast, a particularly fine Darjeeling can take a full minute or more to present all its nuances.

Not so Bancha, Hojicha, and Kukicha. Their toastiness is always attractively simple and forthright, which makes them all popular substitutes for coffee. And they tend to leave a delicate furry sensation on the roof of the mouth, which is, for many people, reason enough to celebrate them.

Tea had come as a deliverer to a land that called for deliverance;
a land of beef and ale, of heavy eating and abundant
drunkenness; of gray skies and harsh winds; of strong-nerved,
stout-purposed, slow-thinking men and women. Above all,
a land of sheltered homes and warm firesides—firesides
that were waiting—waiting, for the bubbling kettle and
the fragrant breath of tea.

AGNES REPPLIER FROM *TO THINK OF TEA*

Bancha

An easy, malleable tea, Bancha has a slightly toasty and woodsy taste, with only a trace amount of caffeine. It has a mellow flavor (which can be intensified with longer brewing) and a yellowish brown liquor—an "everyday drink" if there ever was one. And the health benefits of Bancha are impressive—it contains a hefty amount of calcium, vitamin A, niacin, and iron.

Brewing Bancha

(See The Standard Pot Method on page 30.)

1. Measure 3 teaspoons of tea into an infusion basket.

2. Start heating 3 cups of cold, filtered water in a saucepan.

3. When the Fish Eyes (160°–180°F.) start to break the surface and/or the String of Pearls (180°–190°F.) rim the edge of the pan, pour the water into the teapot.

4. Set the timer for 3 minutes. When the timer sounds, remove the infusion basket and pour into cups.

NOTE: YOU MAY ALSO USE THE STANDARD MUG METHOD ON PAGE 29 OR THE STANDARD *GUYWAN* METHOD ON PAGE 32.

BUYER'S TIP: TRY THE NEAREST JAPANTOWN, HEALTH FOOD STORES, OR MAIL-ORDER CATALOGS TO FIND A GOOD BANCHA.

Brewing Large Quantities

*As with pie crust, everyone hooked on Bancha has his or her little secrets
about how to brew it for optimum flavor. This recipe will produce
a large amount of tea—enough to take to the office.*

1. Measure 1 to 2 tablespoons into a clean, large saucepan.

2. Add 1½ quarts (twelve 6-ounce cups) of filtered water and bring to a boil.

3. Reduce heat and simmer for 2 to 4 minutes.

4. Pour through a strainer into a thermos for convenient all-day drinking.

USER'S TIP: HAVE A THERMOS RESERVED FOR TEA USE ONLY, AS
COFFEE AND OTHER BEVERAGES INTRUDE ON THE TASTE OF THE TEA.

DESSERT BANCHA

When Bancha is brewed "home style" in Japanese households, it can serve as a delightful after-dinner espresso-style beverage. Served in demitasse cups to accompany luscious desserts like a rich apple tart laden with sweet whipped cream, Bancha can be startlingly satisfying.

Brewing Dessert Bancha

1. In a 6- to 8-inch saucepan, pour 6 cups of cold, filtered water.

2. Add ⅓ cup of Bancha.

3. Bring this mixture to a boil, poking at the leaf fragments to ensure they are all saturated.

4. At the boiling point, reduce the heat to the *lowest* simmer point on your stove.

5. Simmer for 10 minutes, or a bit less for a milder tea.

6. Using a large strainer, pour the tea into a heated thermos or thermos/pitcher, and serve in demitasse cups.

USER'S TIP: A FUNNEL IS HELPFUL IN POURING THIS TEA INTO A THERMOS.

Hojicha

*H*ojicha is essentially Bancha that has been roasted a bit longer. Because of its delightfully toasty flavor, many tea drinkers find Hojicha to be very relaxing. Low in caffeine, like all these roasted Japanese greens, it is to my taste more interesting than Bancha or Kukicha.

❦ ❦ ❦ ❦ ❦

*T*he "Down" is our slang for the downstairs dining room at Chez Panisse. Everything there—the food, the service, the ambience—elevates the diner to a place where everything in life becomes rich, understandable, glowing, and balanced. A treasured customer put it nicely by saying, "Halfway through the meal, I just seem to take off."

In quest of a great dessert tea, and to keep the culinary aesthetics high for those Down diners, I asked Roy Fong of the Imperial Tea Court in San Francisco to blend a Hojicha for us, something complex, intense, and strong, but still toasty, delicious, and earthy. I intended to use it as a sort of "tea espresso" for after-dinner drinking.

Roy spent two full days mixing and roasting various blends until he struck the perfect balance. Wanting to give it a wintry, cozy, by-the-fireside kind of name, we considered calling it Winter Hearth, but Roy suggested Kang Cha, *kang* being a kind of horizontal chimney found in humble Chinese homes that one could sit or sleep on—or even use as a table.

The tea was a great success at Chez Panisse, and when happy diners asked to know the meaning of Kang Cha, the waiters had a chance to "show a little charm" as they say in the South, and tell the story of its naming.

Brewing Hojicha

(See The Standard Pot Method on page 30.)

1. Measure 3 teaspoons of dry leaf into an infusion basket.

2. Start heating 3 to 4 cups of cold, filtered water in a saucepan.

3. When the Fish Eyes (160°–180°F.) break the surface and/or the String of Pearls (180°– 190°F.) rims the edge of the pan, pour the water into the teapot.

4. Set the timer for 3 minutes.

5. When the timer sounds, remove the infusion basket and pour the tea.

NOTE: YOU MAY ALSO USE THE STANDARD MUG METHOD ON PAGE 29 OR THE STANDARD *GUYWAN* METHOD ON PAGE 32.

USER'S TIP: AT CHEZ PANISSE, WE KEEP THE DESSERT HOJICHA FROM GROWING TOO STRONG IN THE CUP BY USING THE CLASSIC CHRYSANTHEMUM FLOWER METHOD. A SINGLE DRIED FLOWER IS PRESENTED IN A THIMBLE-SIZE CUP BESIDE THE DRINKING CUP, THE FLOWER TO BE TRANSFERRED TO THE LIQUOR TO ACT AS A SPONGE AND DIFFUSE ITS STRENGTH.

USER'S TIP: AT HOME, HOJICHA, LIKE BANCHA, CAN BE PREPARED AS A DESSERT TEA (SEE RECIPE FOR DESSERT BANCHA ON PAGE 54). IT WILL BE A BIT MELLOWER, MORE COMPLEX, AND QUITE DELICIOUS.

BUYER'S TIP: TRY THE NEAREST JAPANTOWN, MAIL-ORDER CATALOGS, OR HEALTH-ORIENTED GROCERY STORES TO FIND A GOOD HOJICHA.

Kukicha

Made up of the twigs—the actual branches from the last plucking of the season—the flavor of Kukicha is woodsy, but also truly earthy. Not to be confused with Ko-kei-cha, a type of powdered green tea, Kukicha is extremely low in caffeine, a favorite of vegans, and the preferred substitute for coffee for those on a macrobiotic diet. Health food stores and grocery stores specializing in natural foods are usually good sources for Twig Tea—the Anglicized name for Kukicha. Cold or iced Kukicha makes a very nice iced coffee substitute.

My friend Todd decided to become a vegan several years ago. After making the arduous transition away from meat and dairy products and all things greasy and sugary, he found himself still craving that morning kick he used to get from coffee and a big fat cookie. Searching his various vegan and macrobiotic texts, he kept running into references to Twig Tea.

Doubtful that twigs of any sort could give him that good old morning jolt, he nevertheless bravely bought some Kukicha and was delighted to find that in his lean and hungry state, a well-brewed cup of Kukicha was a fabulous, zingy way to start his day.

Brewing Kukicha

(See The Standard Pot Method on page 30.)

1. Measure 3 tablespoons of tea into an infusion basket.

2. Start heating 3 cups of cold filtered water in a saucepan.

3. When you have attained the Turbulent Waters (190°–210°F.) stage, pour the water into the teapot.

4. Set the timer for 3 to 5 minutes, depending on the strength desired.

5. When the timer sounds, remove the infusion basket and pour the tea into cups.

NOTE: YOU MAY ALSO USE THE STANDARD MUG METHOD ON PAGE 29 OR THE STANDARD *GUYWAN* METHOD ON PAGE 32.

SENCHA

(Also known as I-chi Ban Cha, the number one pick)

Sencha is for the Japanese what English Breakfast tea is for the British—ubiquitous, irreplaceable, and reassuring. A staple in most Japanese households, Sencha certainly deserves to be called the "everyday drink" of Japan. Though the neophyte might mistake a Green Yunnan for a Dragon Well, there is no mistaking the classic Sencha flavor—tangy, full-bodied, and evocative of seaweed (in the best sense of that maritime aroma).

This unique tea can prove to be both a blessing and a curse. Brewed correctly, Sencha's tangy, sharp-edged flavor makes a wonderful accompaniment to food, especially grilled seafood and Italian pastas and pizzas. But overbrew it, and Sencha can turn intensely bitter. This same bitterness, sometimes unpleasantly medicinal, may also occur if too much of the dry leaf is used, or if the water is too hot.

Put another way, Sencha is *not* the most forgiving of teas. Indeed, I would wager that overbrewed Sencha is the leading reason why some Westerners have been turned off to the whole array of green teas, since it is often the first green tea they come into contact with. My technique for making Sencha is to focus exclusively on the tea once the water is on the leaf, and to calmly wait one blessed minute for that perfect cup (or pot) to manifest. Leaving the leaf in the water too long is the surest way to spoil your Sencha. Learn to brew it correctly, and Sencha will become a favorite staple in your teatime repertoire.

Around 1987, at Alice's invitation, David Vardy staged a fabulous Japanese dinner at Chez Panisse to promote his new tearoom and restaurant, O Chamé, now a mainstay of the Bay Area cuisine scene. Planning to finish the feast with a delectable Sencha, David found himself confronted with a logistical nightmare—fifty more people than anticipated had come to the party.

Leaping into the fray, I helped David improvise with a canvas pastry bag and a China hat (a large restaurant-size cone-shaped sieve), and we managed to make just enough strong, delicious, and *very* green Sencha for everyone to have a cup.

The next morning, Alice came to work with lowered head and a heavy tread. She'd hardly slept a wink, the Sencha packing a wallop she'd had no idea green tea could deliver. Does green tea have caffeine in it? Far less than coffee, but yes, definitely. That was when I discovered that the stimulating effects of Sencha—and green tea in general—are not limited to the caffeine.

Later on, I would use Sencha's strength and penetrating flavor to good effect by creating a Sencha concentrate and making it available in the upstairs café at Chez Panisse. There the bartender could dispense a non-alcoholic elixir—one part concentrate, three parts water—for those guests wary of wine and weary of vapid mineral waters.

Brewing Sencha

(See The Standard Mug Method on page 29.)

1. Measure 2 teaspoons of dry leaf into a strainer and place in a mug.

2. Start heating 2 to 3 cups of cold, filtered water in a saucepan.

3. When Fish Eyes (160°–180°F.) start to break the surface, pour the water over the leaves.

4. Set the timer for 2 minutes. Do not walk away. Meditate. When the timer sounds, remove the strainer and pour the tea into another mug.

5. Set the timer for 1 more minute.

6. When the timer sounds, begin to drink.

NOTE: YOU MAY ALSO USE THE STANDARD POT METHOD ON PAGE 30 OR THE STANDARD *GUYWAN* METHOD ON PAGE 32.

BUYER'S TIP: START WITH A MEDIUM-PRICED SENCHA. MANY ARE AVAILABLE AT LOCAL ASIAN MARKETS, OR ORDER FROM ONE OF THE MAIL-ORDER HOUSES (PAGE 107).

JASMINE TEAS

Pearl Jasmine — *Yin Hao* — *Middle Grade* — *Restaurant Grade*

There is a system [of tea]. It makes about eight thousand distinctions. Perhaps there are more exceptions to the system than distinctions within it. I have seventy-three years in tea, but I do not know the system. In the West you use an alphabet. In China we learn characters. It is the same with tea.

PROFESSOR ZHUANG, CHAIRMAN OF THE FUJIAN TEA SOCIETY,
FROM JASON GOODWIN'S *A TIME FOR TEA*

Jasmine tea is like champagne. It goes with almost everything, stands alone (a *self-drinker*, in tea talk), and makes both a perfect hostess gift and a fabulous iced tea drink.

Jasmine was "invented" in China during the Ming Dynasty, about A.D. 1500 when flowers were *the* artistic image—figuring in poetry, ceramics, and song. Perhaps that's why jasmine flowers were chosen to give their intoxicating scent to tea leaves. Another reason may have been to cover up a moldy smell due to poor storage.

The tea is made by laying fresh jasmine petals atop the tea leaves, then tea leaves atop more petals, and so on. Up to six layers of blossoms alternating with tea leaves are used to create the highest-quality jasmines, using flowers picked at their aromatic peak. When the jasmine scent is fully merged with the leaves, the petals are removed, and the tea carefully dried again. Leaving the flower petals in the mix risks decay and spoilage.

There are many grades of jasmine. The top grade is Pearl, with Yin Hao a close second. The next level includes a large group of good to mediocre varieties. The lowliest of jasmines fills the tea bags in ordinary Chinese restaurants. It tastes of *something,* but I'm never certain what the flavor actually is. If you open up that little bag, you won't even find a poor-quality green tea; you'll find black tea dust!

In the making of these less expensive teas, the petals are often left in the mix to keep labor costs down, which sometimes results in sickening over-sweetness. A superabundance of jasmine petals in your tea usually means an unpleasantly overpowering flavor and aroma. When you are better acquainted with good jasmines, you will immediately be able to discern the inferior teas by the slightly slimy feel they create on the roof of your mouth.

Pearl Jasmine

(Also known as Shou Kao, pronounced Show Cow)

Pearl Jasmine, the most popular of jasmine teas, is a fairly recent innovation and has swept ahead of the classic Yin Hao in popularity. The "pearls" are made in the same manner as the pellets of Gunpowder. Individual leaves are rolled by hand into tiny balls—each its own little world of flavor. It's the ancient version of our "flavor packet" (to borrow a marketing slogan), and calling it a pearl makes it sound romantic in contrast with the militaristic sounding Gunpowder.

Tea Lore

In ancient times teas were flavored with onions, spices, ginger, and even yak butter—this last providing early northern tribes in China with a nourishing tea-based stew.

Jasmine has always been the most popular flavored tea in the world. Over the years it was followed by Earl Grey (citrus oil), Constant Comment (orange peel), and today's over-the-top combinations of mango-papaya, passionflower-ginger, strawberry-banana, and the most outrageous to my taste—chocolate.

Jasmine tea is a good example of how divine a full-leaf tea can be, and how bad chopped-up little dried bits (known in the trade as dust) can taste— either of nothing at all, or bitter.

Brewing Pearl Jasmine

(See The Standard Guywan Method on page 32.)

1. Place enough pearls to cover the bottom of the cup with a single layer.

2. Start heating about 2 to 3 cups of cold, filtered water until you get Shrimp Eyes (140°–160°F.) When these tiny bubbles cover the bottom of the pan, pour the water into the *guywan*.

3. Cover and wait about a minute until the pearls begin to open, then watch as they settle, stroking the liquid occasionally with the lid.

4. Replace the lid.

5. In 2 to 3 minutes your first sip is ready.

NOTE: YOU MAY ALSO USE THE STANDARD POT METHOD ON PAGE 30 OR THE STANDARD MUG METHOD ON PAGE 29.

USER'S TIP: AS YOUR TASTE EVOLVES, YOU MAY WANT TO TRY USING JUST FIVE OR SIX PEARLS IN THE *GUYWAN* OR GLASS POT. IT'S A DELIGHT TO WATCH THEM LAZILY UNFURL AS THEY FLAVOR THE WATER WITH THEIR LOVELY TASTE.

BUYER'S TIP: MANY SUPERMARKETS WILL HAVE JASMINES THAT ARE PLEASANT, IF NOT SPECTACULAR. IT'S FUN TO GET SUCH BASIC JASMINES TO ACCOMPANY A TAKE-OUT CHINESE DINNER. BUT IF YOU WANT A FULL, MOOD-ALTERING EXPERIENCE, GO TO A TEA SHOP AND BUY THE MOST EXPENSIVE YIN HAO OR PEARL. MAIL-ORDER CATALOGS ALSO PROVIDE WONDERFUL JASMINES WHEN YOU BUY THE TOP OF THE LINE.

The main business office at Chez Panisse is a series of rooms in a modern apartment that sprang up adjacent to the restaurant—originally a farmhouse built in 1904. In the kitchen of the apartment, commonly served teas are stored in a cupboard where it's dry and cool. But the most expensive teas are stored in an unmarked spot and are off-limits to staff. Among these special teas is Pearl Jasmine.

Alice likes to present friends and honored guests with table bouquets, and these flowers are kept in the office, awaiting their debut in the main dining room. Add to this the frequent floral tributes to Alice arriving from near and far, and you'll understand why the room is so often a festive and fragrant place.

One day I entered the busy office and smelled something heavenly—something like the scent of Hawaii. I looked all over, but saw no flowers. I peeked around the corner into Alice's office, and then into the manager's office. No flowers.

"Where is that gorgeous scent coming from?" I asked. Everyone shrugged. Then, from one of the desks ringing the room, a young woman—a new employee—looked up through a set of very sophisticated eyelashes and sheepishly pointed to a teapot by her side. "It's me," she said. "It's the Pearl Jasmine. I'm sorry."

I stopped short, then laughed and demanded a sip. She'd brewed it perfectly. What a tea!

Yin Hao

Yin Hao translates as Silver Down, referring to the soft, fuzzy, whitish, hairy underside of the leaf, indicating its newness and freshness—a major component of its superior flavor. These most delicate and aromatic jasmine flowers are left where they are harvested, and the tea leaves brought to them so their integrity is preserved—exactly the opposite of the usual method for creating ordinary jasmines, wherein the petals travel to the tea leaves.

In the 1980s Yin Hao was a great favorite of the fictional James Bond, adding some popularity and glamour to this classic tea.

Brewing Yin Hao

(See The Standard Pot Method on page 30.)

1. Measure 3 teaspoons of dry leaf into an infusion basket.

2. Start heating 3 cups of cold, filtered water.

3. When Fish Eyes (160°–180°F.) start to break the surface, or String of Pearls (180°–190°F.) *just* begin to rim the edge of the pan, pour the water into the teapot.

4. Set the timer for 1 to 2 minutes.

5. When the timer sounds, remove the infusion basket.

6. Pour the tea into your favorite cups.

NOTE: YOU MAY ALSO USE THE STANDARD MUG METHOD ON PAGE 29 OR THE STANDARD *GUYWAN* METHOD ON PAGE 32.

USER'S TIP: YIN HAO, LIKE ALL JASMINES, VARIES IN SWEETNESS AND STRENGTH, SO EACH BATCH YOU BUY WILL REQUIRE A LITTLE FINE-TUNING UNTIL YOU FIND A BALANCE OF LEAF QUANTITY TO BREWING TIME THAT SUITS YOU.

USER'S TIP: FOR YIN HAO, WHEN IN DOUBT, UNDERBREW AND UNDERBOIL.

BUYER'S TIP: THE SECOND AND THIRD GRADES OF YIN HAO ARE CHUN FENG (SPRING WIND) AND CHUNG HAO (SPRING DOWN).

Installing a New Tea at Chez Panisse

For the person in charge of buying and installing a new tea (or coffee or wine) at a fine restaurant, the moment of installation is a big one, though it often slips into the scheme of things with the tiniest of ripples as far as the staff and the patrons are concerned. I adore the term install *and conjured it up one day after much thought and negotiation and tasting. To get a tea on the shelf at Chez Panisse is an arduous journey from seeing the need for a certain tea, to its actual selection, and then to the moment of putting it on the shelf for daily use.*

The process involves choosing the name of the tea for the menu, getting the restaurant manager to approve the price, making sure the name is spelled correctly on the computer, arranging for its proper double-sealed storage canister, explaining its preparation to the bussers, passing out samples of the properly brewed tea to waiters and cooks, and generally hovering over it like an anxious mother over a kindergartner.

The moment on a quiet Tuesday afternoon when I physically placed the large, shining can-

ister on the shelf, I thought, Ah! There it is. At last installed," *and turned to acknowledge the grateful applause. No one was there. One languid busboy finally appeared and asked,* "Whaz this?" *and ambled off. That was it.*

Selecting a tea that will taste good and survive the abuse of sometimes very hurried preparation, checking its keeping qualities and its availability, ensuring its dependable on-time arrival from the vendor, and hoping no other restaurant has a similar kind of tea quite as good —all that is what makes my inner teakettle boil.

That's the practical side of getting a tea installed, and then there's the aesthetic side of the process. Is the new tea an exciting, intriguing, tasty one that will marry well with the sometimes delicate, sometimes vigorous Italian-French, Alice-inspired foods of Chez Panisse?

Customers often fall in love with the supporting accompaniments to the main dishes— the bread, the butter, the olive oil, the coffee, the wine, the tea. These little extras become *the restaurant to that person, and they want to take them home. That's why that brand of tea or wine or bread* must *be available.*

The Muddled
Middle-Class Jasmines

*A*mong the great number of midpriced jasmines carried in health food stores and supermarkets, you'll find row upon row of unfamiliar brands of boxed jasmine tea. It is wise to look at the ingredient label—remember that the term *natural flavors* serves as an unregulated dumping ground for any kind of flavor, including chemically produced ones. A good rule of thumb for medium-priced jasmines is to buy the one with the fewest additives.

Because jasmine's flavor is so pronounced, sometimes a sloppily or even weakly brewed one can taste "pretty good." If you want to use the bagged variety, look on page 84 for directions. For brewing loose-leaf jasmines, follow the standard directions for green teas on pages 29–32. Within two or three tries you'll be able to make the little adjustments to suit your palate.

THE FINER GREEN TEAS

*In tea
the best
is
most economical.*

—FROM A LIPTON TEA BOOKLET
PUBLISHED IN 1934

Fine green tea is not expensive (and it's delicious!).

 Tea that costs $120 per pound = a dollar per pot.

Tea that costs $80 dollars a pound = 66 cents per pot.

Two ounces of fine tea will make 40 cups of tea, with two to three steepings per cup!

If you use tea that costs $100 per pound, it will cost $2.40 to fill a wine bottle—a quarter of the cost of a ho-hum Chardonnay.

DRAGON WELL

(Also known as Longching, pronounced Lung Jing)

*D*ragon Well is the Tiffany of green teas, and more has been written about this pinnacle event tea than any other. The adjectives are running out. The only way I can begin to describe a great Dragon Well is to say it tastes like the very essence of a lush spring meadow drenched in morning dew, mingled with the scents of rich black earth, roses, and honeysuckle. Imagine imbibing—not inhaling, not smelling, but actually *drinking*—such a liquid. Once you taste a great Dragon Well, the only problem you'll have will be keeping it in stock and paying attention to other green teas.

The "well" is an actual spring-fed well (a circular stone enclosure where the water is gathered) with a temple and a teahouse nearby—not far from Hangshou. Legend has it that during a severe drought a resident monk summoned up a lucky dragon he'd heard was in the neighborhood. He prayed, and lo, the rains came, the crops were saved, and the peasants rejoiced.

Tigers (also good luck) get into a second legend. Another drought dried up the spring that fed the well, and soon thereafter, miraculously, two tigers appeared and began to dash back and forth near the spring, causing the water to gush forth anew—as it continues to gush to this day. Since then the spring has been called Tiger Run Spring, and the name has been affixed to certain lesser teas.

Drinking Dragon Well made from the first flush (the first spring picking), with water from *the* well, is said to be the ultimate tea drinker's experience. When Chairman Mao Tse-tung met with President Nixon for the first time, the tea they drank was Dragon Well, and it was in springtime, in the teahouse, near the temple. Did Nixon grasp the honor? I wonder. But words fail. This tea demands to be drunk rather than talked about.

Language Lesson

In the restaurant world, the life, the staff, and the lingo can shift very quickly. Mario Daniele, the new general manager at Chez Panisse, told me to contact Lee Ann, our personnel manager, about shaping up the tea service. Lee Ann Phillips started our conversation by saying, "Alang will be the most help to you in making good, efficient tea service."

Aha, I thought, envisioning a glamorous, Middle Eastern young man. I dashed to the downstairs bussers' station and asked for Alang. I got puzzled looks. Since the staff was changing rapidly, I let it go and went upstairs and got the same response.

Then, a very tall, statuesque busperson walked by and someone asked her, "Are you short today?"

"No," she replied, "I'm *a long.*"

I closed my mouth, looked wise, checked the schedule for Chez Panisse's more exclusive downstairs restaurant, and sure enough, the more experienced bussers had longer shifts.

Restaurant life—I love it!

Brewing Dragon Well

(See The Standard Guywan Method on page 32.)

*One can make Dragon Well in a pot, but it and other superior teas taste best in the covered cup (**guywan**) because you will have more control over the proportion of water to leaf. The intimacy of the act—the closeness of your nose to the fragrant leaf—is quite appealing.*

1. Cover the bottom of the *guywan* with a shallow layer of the dry leaf, approximately 1 teaspoon.

2. Start heating 2 to 3 cups of cold, filtered water in a saucepan.

3. When you see the Fish Eyes (160°–180°F.) breaking the surface, the water is ready to pour.

4. Pour the water into the *guywan*.

5. Let the leaves rest for a minute or so, then stroke the water with the lid (or with a soup-spoon). Replace the lid.

6. In another minute or so, you can begin to drink.

7. When you have finished one cup, add more hot water directly, as is, from the saucepan.

NOTE: YOU MAY ALSO USE THE STANDARD POT METHOD ON PAGE 30 OR THE STANDARD MUG METHOD ON PAGE 29.

BUYER'S TIP: REMEMBER THAT PRICE REFLECTS QUALITY. YOU MIGHT WANT TO START YOUR DRAGON WELL ADVENTURE BY BUYING 2 OUNCES, ABOUT ELEVEN DOLLARS' WORTH, IN THE NEXT-TO-BEST RANGE. THE TOP GRADE IS CALLED QING MING.

USER'S TIP: HOW HOT YOU MAKE THE WATER FOR THE SECOND OR THIRD POURING IS A MATTER OF YOUR MOOD AT THE MOMENT. WITH A SUPERIOR TEA, IT'S UP TO YOU. YOUR THIRD INFUSION WILL TASTE QUITE WONDERFUL WITH WHATEVER TEMPERATURE YOU CHOOSE SO AS LONG AS YOU USE WATER BEFORE IT HAS BOILED.

USER'S TIP: DRAGON WELL IS FAMOUS FOR ITS PALE GREEN HUE, BEST SET OFF BY A WHITE CUP OR A CLEAR GLASS TUMBLER. IF THE DRY LEAF LOOKS YELLOWISH, THE TEA IS PROBABLY STALE. IF IT WAS PURCHASED RECENTLY, RETURN IT.

DONG DING

(Also called Tung Ting)
"Cold Top" or "Frozen Summit"

*T*echnically an oolong, but a very green one, Dong Ding is also known as Jade Oolong, Green Oolong, and sometimes just Oolong. Cold Top refers to the mountains where this tea first grew in Mainland China. Now the name Dong Ding (so much fun to say—just Ding Dong backward) is thought of as a generic type. The aroma, as my tea mentor Norwood Pratt says, is "delicate, but far more pronounced than any green tea." As Burgundy wines are grown in many places other than Burgundy, the same is true for Dong Ding. Oolongs were transplanted to Taiwan from China in 1850 and immediately became popular with tea drinkers in the United States. Around the turn of the last century, a Formosa (Taiwan) oolong was *the* stylish and delicious sensation. Be sure, for my sake, to try the Taiwanese variety.

Brewing Dong Ding

(See The Standard Guywan Method on page 32.)

*Pretend you are sitting across the table from me as we examine a leaf
of my favorite green tea. It is most certainly green—a rich, mossy green—and
looks as if a tiny gnome had taken the leaf and scrunched it up in his fist. When this
leaf opens up in the first pouring, it begins to exude its extraordinary flavor, as palpable
as a food—not just a tea. Think of Dong Ding as Yo Yo Ma opening up full volume
on the cello. Dong Ding fills the mouth—warm and satisfying—and it can be felt
throughout the whole body. The flavor seems somehow round, and it is fun to
examine the used leaves that display the famous two leaves and a bud.*

1. Cover the bottom of the *guywan* with a shallow layer of
   the dry leaf, approximately 1 teaspoon.

2. Start heating 2 to 3 cups of cold, filtered water in a
   saucepan.

3. When you see the Fish Eyes (160°–180°F.) breaking the
   surface, the water is ready to pour.

4. Pour the water into the *guywan*.

5. Let the leaves rest for a minute or so, then stroke the water
   with the lid (or with a soupspoon). Replace the lid.

6. In another minute or so, you can begin to drink.

7. When you have finished one cup, add more hot water
   directly, as is, from the saucepan.

CONTINUED

NOTE: You may also use The Standard Pot Method on page 30 or The Standard Mug Method on page 29.

USER'S TIP: This tea produces great taste even with a third round of hot water. To my palate, the second steeping tastes fullest.

BUYER'S TIP: Examine the leaf before you buy. Leaves may vary in size, but all Dong Dings are rolled into crumpled balls (not the tight, spherical balls of Gunpowder) and are a rich, mossy green.

BI LUO CHUN

(Also called Pi lo Chun)
"Green Snail Spring"

*T*he good flavor of Luo Chun (pronounced Bee Low Chun) reminds me of the reedy quality of Benny Goodman's clarinet playing and is one of those special teas loved by connoisseurs and ordinary folk alike. It *is* special. Each pound of tea contains sixty to seventy thousand sets of the bud and the accompanying half-opened leaf. Like other wonderfully complex teas, the flavors present one layer after another. Tea people go on and on when they try to describe their favorite Bi Luo Chun—and then they tell you where to buy it. Bi Luo Chun's trademark is a remarkable fresh aroma and taste—like the whiff of pine trees in the distance.

The flavor? Hard to say. A good Bi Luo Chun should have a delicacy to it, but with the hint of an edge—a slightly reedy quality—strong, vigorous, and sweet. Bi Luo Chun is like an old tune played by a master—made new through genius.

Brewing Bi Luo Chun

(See The Standard Guywan Method on page 32.)

Brewing Bi Luo Chun is a delicate procedure, but the results are rewarding. If you enjoy Dragon Well, you'll also enjoy Bi Luo Chun. The temperature for brewing must be even lower than for Dragon Well (see recipe below). These two famous teas are almost always paired together in catalogs and stores. Once you become a Bi Luo Chun fan, it's hard to explore other green teas with enthusiasm.

1. Cover the bottom of the *guywan* with a shallow layer of the dry leaf, approximately 1 teaspoon.

2. Start heating 2 to 3 cups of cold, filtered water in a saucepan.

3. When you see the Fish Eyes (160°–180°F.) breaking the surface, the water is ready to pour.

4. Pour the water into the *guywan*.

5. Let the leaves rest for a minute or so, then stroke the water with the lid (or with a soupspoon). Replace the lid.

6. In another minute or so, you can begin to drink.

7. When you have finished one cup, add more hot water directly, as is, from the saucepan.

NOTE: YOU MAY ALSO USE THE STANDARD POT METHOD ON PAGE 30 OR THE STANDARD MUG METHOD ON PAGE 29.

USER'S TIP: A clear glass tumbler can be used as well as a *guywan,* and is often preferred for Bi Luo Chun in order to appreciate the color of the liquor and to enjoy watching the spiraling descent of the leaves.

BUYER'S TIP: Bi Luo Chuns from Taiwan have a fuller, more robust taste than those from Mainland China and are a better value.

BUYER'S TIP: The dry leaves of high-quality Bi Luo Chun are tiny, delicate, and twisted (curvy), and appear not to weigh much, as if you'd like to toss them in the air and watch them fall. I'm referring to the most expensive ones, but remember, they will always taste better than the lower-priced ones. The finer Bi Luo Chuns can take two, three, or four pourings of hot water.

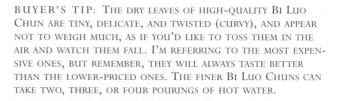

One spring evening at Chez Panisse, after supper on the small porch of the upstairs café, Norwood Pratt, Roy and Grace Fong, and I started sampling Bi Luo Chun. It was that delicious time of day when the gold-pink light of sunset filtered through the small lavender panes and the ginkgo tree cast its dramatic shadows on the newly laid tables—the fresh, white linens giving off their own light.

I wondered aloud why Bi Luo Chun was always translated as "Green Snail Spring." The leaf is tightly twisted in corkscrew fashion, but doesn't look at all like a fat snail. As we watched the leaves spiraling to the bottom of the cup, Grace Fong smiled and said, "You know, the Chinese character for *snail* is also the character for *spiral.*"

Ah! At last. The mystery solved. And we began to sip the delicate and delicious tea as the light began to fade.

TEA BAGS

In 1908, tea importer Thomas Sullivan began sending out his samples to tea shops in little silk bags, instead of in more expensive tins, and he was soon flooded with orders—his buyers insisting he continue to send the tea in bags. To his surprise, he discovered that people were dunking the entire bag in the cup or pot instead of untying the bag and sampling the tea in the usual way. Shortly thereafter, he substituted gauze for the silk because it was much more economical.

The tea bag was created as a convenience, and that's just what it is. It's also an inexpensive and readily available item for a green tea neophyte to try. Tea professionals tend to call tea bags "beverages" rather than honor them with the title of Tea, but I do use them on occasion and find them to be a lifesaver sometimes. On a long airline flight they are a real boon.

I have two or three favorites. Lipton is at the top of the list because it is blended with enough complexity and skill (as is Lipton black tea) to provide a cheering, sturdy, smooth cup when brewed with two bags. When brewed with one bag, a sweet, delicate cup emerges, making a nice accompaniment to a simple cookie or a piece of white toast.

Yamamotoyama is also a favored brand of mine. Their teas are sealed tightly in foil and blended in a straightforward way. They have a very clear, clean taste—not at all comparable to fine loose-leaf varieties—yet they still produce a pleasing, light, and refreshing drink.

I have others to recommend, too, that will provide an introduction to green tea and are for most of us easy to tuck into a pocket as a traveling panacea.

Standard Tea Bag Method

1. Heat cold, filtered water in a saucepan until you see tiny, pinpoint-size bubbles covering the bottom of the pan.

2. Place the tea bag in the cup.

3. Pour the water over the bag, and brew for 1 minute only.

4. Remove the bag and allow 1 to 4 minutes before drinking. The flavor will improve in the cup.

Helen's Tea Bag Guide

The following teas are the tastiest, most available, and dependably consistent. I have tested all of them, and my brewing instructions do not always agree with the instructions given on the packages.

1. Lipton
2. Choice
3. Twinings
4. Triple Leaf
5. Traditional Medicinals
6. Trader Joe's
7. Alavita
8. Yamamotoyama
9. Bigelow Teas Green Tea

Brewing Tea with Lipton Bags

The First Way

For a delicate "afternoon" cup you will need a teacup, a saucepan, and one bag.

1. Heat cold, filtered water until you see pinpoint-size bubbles on the bottom of the pan.
2. Place the bag in a teacup and pour the water over it.
3. Keep the bag in the cup for no more than 30 seconds.
4. Remove the bag.
5. Wait 1 minute and drink.

The Second Way

*For a clean, sturdy, smooth, bracing mugful—to accompany a hearty meal—
you will need a large mug, a saucepan, and two tea bags.*

1. Heat cold, filtered water until you see pinpoint-size bubbles on the bottom of the pan.
2. Place two bags in a large mug and pour water over them.
3. Keep the bags in the mug for 1 minute only.
4. Remove the bags.
5. Wait at least 3 minutes and drink.

Brewing Tea with Choice Bags

Follow the directions on the box

Brewing Tea with Twinings Bags

Follow the suggestions for Lipton bags.

Brewing Tea with Triple Leaf Bags

Follow the directions on the packet.
Do not try a two-bag method.

Brewing Tea with Traditional Medicinals Bags

Follow the directions on the box.

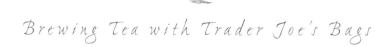

Brewing Tea with Trader Joe's Bags

Follow the directions on the can.
This will yield a minimally bitter,
very assertive cup.

Brewing Tea with Alavita Bags

These bags can be found in almost
every health food store. Follow the
instructions on the packet.

Brewing Tea with Yamamotoyama Bags
(for Green and Gen Mai Cha)

Follow the directions on the packet
exactly. Both teas yield true but lean
versions of the same teas when
brewed with loose-leaf versions.

BUYER'S TIP: BEWARE OF THE TERM *NATURAL FLAVORS* ON
BOXES OF TEA BAGS! THAT TERM (SANCTIONED BY THE FDA) IS A
DUMPING GROUND FOR ADDITIVES THAT APE NATURAL FLAVORS
BUT ARE ACTUALLY SYNTHETICALLY PRODUCED.

BUYER'S TIP: FOR THAT LONG AIRLINE FLIGHT, TAKE ALONG
BAGS FROM LIPTON OR TRIPLE LEAF TEAS. THE LIPTON WILL
YIELD FLAVOR WITH ANY TEMPERATURE OF WATER, AND THE
TRIPLE LEAF WILL NEVER GET BITTER.

*I*n my first weeks as tea buyer (as well as hostess) at Chez Panisse in 1981, I got a call from a man at a large tea company, saying he wanted to call on me and offer me their tea. At the time, the restaurant was beginning to get considerable press and was being hailed as the most important new restaurant on the American scene. "I'm coming!" he yelled. "I'm taking a plane tomorrow—may I have an appointment?"

The next day he roared up the café stairs, assistant in tow, and began extolling the value and excellence of his elaborate sample case.

I sniffed trouble—why wasn't he talking about the tea? Then he opened it, and all three of us gazed at the beautifully arranged tray of tea bags.

I stammered and explained that we would never consider tea bags. The assistant was indignant. Turning to his superior, he actually said in front of me, "But you told me we had the finest tea in America."

The scene began to disintegrate. I remained seated but truly wanted to flee. "Well," he sighed, "where do you keep your tea? I'd like to see it."

I had just begun my tea work at the café and was not aware that tea should be stored in lightproof containers. I gestured limply to the rear of the restaurant. "Oh, I have a few Mason jars in the back." It was the truth. We had very few teas to offer in the beginning; almost nothing in the café was very pinned down yet (one of the owners literally ran the day-to-day operations from a few slips of paper in his wallet).

Mr. Tea Company looked absolutely crestfallen. I felt so sorry for him, and I was so uninitiated in the restaurant world, that I mentioned a delicatessen down the street I thought might be interested in his tea. He paled and told me that he was the vice-president of his company and did not make sales calls.

We ended with several mutually embarrassed handshakes, and I stumbled back to work.

THE BOTTLE
AND CAN SCENE

*T*here aren't many *pure* green teas available in this category. Most bottled and canned teas contain so much sugar that they belong in the soda-pop world.

In Asian markets, sushi restaurants, and Asian take-out spots, you'll be able to find some sugar-free green teas in bottles or cans. The most widely available brand is Itoen. It contains purified water, green tea, and vitamin C. Also available in cans is Pooka brand, which contains green tea, vitamin C, and sodium bicarbonate. E-BEN brand comes in bottles and contains only green tea and water. Finally, there's a brand called Honestea, which is widely available on the East Coast.

TEA AS HOUSEHOLD HELPER

For houseplants: Leftover tea liquor can be diluted and poured on them every third watering, and on outdoor plants, too. Spent leaves make fine mulch for plants, both indoors and out.

For a hard-surfaced floor: Toss dried used tea leaves on the floor, then sweep. The leaves become the old-fashioned janitor's helper.

Washing a straw purse, a straw place mat, or a straw floor covering in a strong tea solution will whisk away odors, and the surface will look fresh again.

Pincushions and pillows: Used tea leaves that have been completely dried can be used to stuff pincushions and pillows. There will be no noticeable odor remaining in the dried leaves.

For cleaning Oriental rugs: Sprinkle damp tea leaves over the entire rug. Wait a few minutes, then vacuum or sweep them up.

Tea as Dye

The town of Cambrai in France gained world renown at the end of the nineteenth century for its production of a light, soft, creamy tan fabric known in the English-speaking world as cambric. At about this same time, the phenomenon known as Children's Tea was all the rage in England—a tea made with more milk than tea to lessen the stimulating effect of the beverage on the kiddies. The liquid resulting from all this milk added to a little black tea was a light tan color and came to be known as cambric tea.

It was also at this historic juncture, give or take a decade or two, that ladies of Victorian England found that by dipping their dainty white fabrics—camisoles and underwear and the like—in tea, they could achieve an alluring creamy tan color. And so it came to pass that an overheated British officer serving in steamy India, tired of wearing his heavy regulation-issue trousers, sought relief by wearing his pure white, lightweight pajama bottoms instead. However, to make these flimsy trousers

more acceptable to the discerning eyes of his fellows, he dipped them in tea, which turned them cambric tan, and the world's beloved khakis were born.

Fast-forward a hundred years. Alice Waters and her daughter, Fanny, were preparing to leave for an elegant event in Manhattan. Alice's gown was an enchanting ecru (light tan), complete with a drippy lace headband with aqua beading, in which she appeared to have stepped right out of a Maxfield Parrish masterpiece.

Fanny's dress, on the other hand, was dead white cotton lace—something from a 1950s General Electric washing machine ad. What to do about the mismatch? I dipped Fanny's dress in double-strength black tea, and in a twinkling we had two Maxfield Parrish beauties ready to wow New York.

Warning: If you're going to try any tea-dyeing such as this, be sure to thoroughly wet the fabric to be dyed first, and be sure that it is spot-free.

GREEN TEA RECIPES

*T*here are many recipes employing green tea as an ingredient, but in most cases the tea seems more a novelty inclusion than an essential ingredient. The following recipes are built upon the resilient flavors unique to green tea. Unless otherwise noted, use Sencha or another hearty green tea when green tea is called for in a recipe. Save the finer, more expensive green teas for your drinking pleasure.

A Note about Matcha: Green Tea Powder

*M*atcha, the Japanese word for powdered green tea, is the tea used in the famous Japanese tea ceremony. Because its preparation is complex and involves a large number of specialized utensils, I have not included Matcha as one of the *drinking* teas in this book. However, as you will see, powder is invaluable for adding green tea flavor to recipes. The quickest and surest way to purchase green tea powder is to order from any of the larger mail-order houses, or you might be able to find it in an upscale Asian market. Generally speaking, the more you pay for your powder, the better it will taste. (Upton Imports is a good source.)

Ochazuke

Ochazuke, which means "soaked in tea," is a healthy Japanese rice and tea soup. Pouring green tea over rice, with a little nori seaweed crumbled in, began as an informal custom that evolved into a delightful dish with infinite variations.

INGREDIENTS

1 cup hot cooked rice

2 ounces sushi-grade quality of your favorite white-fleshed fish, raw

Wasabi horseradish, finely grated, or paste

½ sheet nori seaweed

1 cup of your favorite hot Japanese green tea

Place the hot rice in a big bowl. Cut the raw fish into paper-thin strips and place on top of the rice. Grate or smear wasabi horseradish onto the fish. Crumble nori over the fish and rice. Pour hot tea on the rice. Serve immediately. Mix with chopsticks or spoon.

WARNING: WASABI CAN BE TOO MUCH OF A BURN FOR SOME PEOPLE, SO START WITH A LITTLE AND ADD MORE FOR DESIRED POTENCY.

VARIATIONS: Mix and match any of the following toppings. Amounts are not critical for this home-style dish.

- Salmon, baked and crumbled into pieces
- Bok choy, washed and thinly sliced
- Carrots, washed and grated
- Radishes, watercress, cabbage
- Japanese pickled plums

NOTE: IF USING LEFTOVER COLD RICE, THE USUAL TOPPINGS ARE PICKLES OR NORI, PROBABLY BECAUSE THESE ARE STAPLES IN MOST JAPANESE KITCHENS.

Green Tea Sauce for Ice Cream

The charming little restaurant Cha-Ya sits a few blocks down Shattuck from Chez Panisse. Everything served at Cha-Ya is vegetarian and exceedingly fresh and flavorful. The proprietor and chef, Atsushi Katsumata, was good enough to share the recipe for his magical sauce with me.

INGREDIENTS

3 tablespoons arrowroot flour

1/2 cup water

3 tablespoons honey

3 tablespoons Matcha (powdered green tea)

Dissolve the arrowroot flour in a small amount of water. Mix well by gradually adding the full amount of water. Strain this mixture to remove undissolved particles of flour. Cook over a low flame while constantly stirring until the mixture turns more or less transparent—about 10 minutes. Cool. Add the honey and the Matcha and mix in a blender until thoroughly blended.

NOTE: YOU MAY SUBSTITUTE CORNSTARCH FOR ARROWROOT FLOUR, AND MAPLE SUGAR FOR HONEY.

Green Tea Granita

This is a delightfully refreshing treat that can be served as a palate cleanser
(serves 6 to 8) or as a dessert (serves 4 to 6).

INGREDIENTS

¼ cup granulated sugar

1½ cups water

1 tablespoon Matcha (powdered
green tea)

2 tablespoons cold water

In a saucepan combine the sugar and 1½ cups water, and bring the mixture to a boil, stirring until the sugar is dissolved. Place the Matcha in a small cup and add 2 tablespoons cold water, 1 tablespoon at a time, stirring to make a thin paste. Remove the saucepan from the heat and stir the Matcha paste into the sugar syrup. Cool. Pour into a 9 × 13-inch metal pan. Freeze this mixture, stirring and crushing the lumps every 30 minutes. After 2 hours, allow the mixture to freeze solid. Using a fork, scrape the granita down the length of the pan, creating icy flakes. Scoop these flakes into a serving bowl.

NOTE: GRANITA CAN BE MADE A DAY AHEAD OF SERVING. ALSO, THE AMOUNT OF SUGAR CAN BE ADJUSTED TO TASTE. AN EXTRA ¼ CUP OF SUGAR MAKES A SWEETER DESSERT GRANITA.

Green Tea Pound Cake

Although buttery dishes don't usually go with green tea, this modern variant on a popular Southern cake does. Commonly served at funerals, the original recipe called for rose geranium leaves to impart a subtle flavor to the cake. Here the subtle flavor is of green tea.

INGREDIENTS

3 cups all-purpose flour

1 teaspoon salt

$1/2$ teaspoon baking powder

$1/2$ teaspoon baking soda

$1/2$ pound butter, softened

2 cups sugar

4 eggs, at room temperature

1 teaspoon vanilla

3 to 4 tablespoons Green Tea Ice Cream Sauce (page 94)

$7/8$ cup buttermilk, at room temperature

Preheat oven to 350°F. Grease an 8-inch Bundt pan. Be sure the ingredients are at room temperature.

Place the flour, salt, baking powder, and baking soda in a large bowl. Sit down. Put the bowl in your lap, then stir and lift the flour mixture, letting it drop back into the bowl from a height of 5 inches. Do this for 3 minutes.

In another bowl, using an electric mixer on high speed, beat the softened butter and sugar together until fluffy and pale yellow. This will take about 5 minutes. At low speed, beat in the eggs, 1 at a time. Add the vanilla and the green tea ice cream sauce and gently blend in.

Stirring by hand, alternately add the flour mixture and the buttermilk to the butter, sugar, and egg mixture, mixing just enough to incorporate each addition. Overmixing now will cause the cake to fall when it is baked. When all ingredients are combined, tilt the bowl and give the batter about 10 quick lifting strokes with the spatula. This incorporates some air into the batter.

Transfer the batter into the cake pan. Smooth the top of the batter with your fingers or a spatula and place the pan in the center of the oven. Bake for exactly 1 hour. The cake is done when the top has turned a golden brown and split open, and a wooden skewer pierced into it comes out clean. Place the cake in the pan on a rack to cool for 5 minutes. Then invert it onto a cake plate and let it cool for at least 30 minutes.

Serve with Gen Mai Cha, Sencha, or even a delicate Dragon Well.

Covered tightly with plastic wrap and stored in the refrigerator, the cake should last 5 to 6 days.

Robert's Green Tea Poached Halibut with Yellow Onions, Fennel Root, and Tarragon

Surprisingly, this is one of the few recipes where the flavor of the green tea emerges in the final result.

SERVES 4

INGREDIENTS

1 tablespoon Sencha or other green tea leaves

1½ cups cold water

1½ tablespoons high-quality peanut oil

2 medium yellow onions, coarsely chopped

1 cup fennel root, coarsely chopped

2 carrots, coarsely chopped

1 tablespoon fresh tarragon, chopped

¼ teaspoon salt

1 pound halibut or comparable firm fish, 4 filets or steaks

Mix the green tea leaves with the cold water. Let the mixture sit for 30 minutes. Strain, reserving the liquid.

In a deep skillet, heat the peanut oil. Add the onions, fennel root, and carrots. Cook over medium heat until the onions are soft, about 10 minutes Add tarragon and salt.

Raise heat to high. Add 1 cup of the reserved tea liquid. Bring to a boil. Place the pieces of fish on top of the vegetable mixture.

Reduce to a simmer. Cook uncovered for 1 hour. Don't worry, the halibut will not disintegrate as it absorbs the tea flavor, and this length of time will allow the tea liquid to reduce to a tasty broth. If the mixture begins to boil dry, add more of the reserved liquid. Approximately half of the liquid should be boiled away by the end of the hour.

Adjust the seasoning. Place the fish on heated plates. Cover with the vegetable mixture. Garnish with a little fresh tarragon.

GLOSSARY

AGONY OF THE LEAVES
The swirling and twisting of the tea leaves
when the water is applied.

BLACK
Tea that has been highly oxidized and well roasted.

CHUNG
Cantonese for *guywan*
(the Mandarin word for a covered cup).

COMPLEX
A tea with many layers of flavor.

EVERYDAY DRINK
A tea that is not very complex or expensive.

FANNINGS
Tiny bits of dried tea, so tiny as to be fanned away
by the small-size sorting machine.

GREEN
Tea that has been oxidized for a short time and briefly fired.

GUYWAN
The three-piece covered cup invented
and used primarily in China.

INFUSION
An extract obtained by steeping a substance in water.

LIQUOR
The liquid obtained by brewing tea leaves in hot water.

OOLONG
Tea that falls somewhere between green and black in
terms of amount of oxidation and roasting time.

ORDINAIRE
An ordinary, everyday tea.

OXIDATION
Exposure of the tea leaves to air.

SELF-DRINKER
A tea that stands alone and needs no additions.
Better than an everyday tea.

SILVER DOWN
The light-colored, fine hairy growth
on the underside of the tea leaf.

TETSUBIN
Japanese cast-iron teapot.

TIP, TIPPY
The tiny budding leaf prized for freshness of flavor.

TISANE
French word for an herbal "tea," an herbal infusion.

TWO LEAVES AND A BUD
The most prized pluck of the tea plant.

YIXING
An area in northeast China one hundred miles west of Shanghai,
and also the name of clays from the area—especially good for
hand-molding into exotic teapots. Also spelled *I-xing*.

ZHONG
A fairly recent invention—the Chinese adaptation
of the covered cup to suit American style.

ORDERING TEA
THROUGH THE MAIL

I'm frequently asked where "good green teas" can be bought. Tea seekers in big cities as well as small towns ask the same question. I usually suggest that for a person living in a large urban area it's no problem to find a tea shop or a tea and coffee specialty store where you can ask questions and find some good basic green teas.

The usual response to that suggestion is "But the clerks are so busy, and I'm not really sure what to ask for."

If it's any consolation, tea executives and phone order takers I've interviewed claim that almost everyone faces this same challenge. The good news is that most order takers at the better mail-order houses are well trained and ready to help. They want your business, and they want you to be happy, so in most cases they will do their best to give you satisfaction.

Don't be shy. After a few minutes of toll-free conversation, they'll take your credit card number, and a few days later the good green leaves will arrive at your door.

Key Descriptive Words

These are terms that may help you as you try to describe teas that you have tasted and enjoyed:

For Japanese teas: *grassy, seaweedy, fishy, haylike*

For Chinese teas: *flowery, sweet, herbaceous, slight vegetable flavor*

The term *flowery* can be broken down further into *rose, jasmine,* or *general*

For teas from green-growing areas in India: *pungent, fruity*

How Much to Buy?

Some catalogs list their amounts in grams. This can be confusing for folks used to thinking in ounces or fractions of a cup. Here is a simple conversion chart of grams to ounces.

125 grams = 4.4 ounces = ¼ pound

250 grams = 8.8 ounces = ½ pound

500 grams = 17 ounces = 1.1 pounds

To make a good two-cup pot of tea requires about 4 grams. A four-cup pot requires 9 grams.

When ordering by mail, don't be shy about asking the order taker to help you understand the amounts you're buying.

Keepability

A good rule of thumb for consuming green tea is not to let it sit around. Brew it as soon as possible after you get it. Remember: the smaller the packet, the faster the tea dries out and loses its freshness.

Sample Packets

Many telephone order takers will recommend that neophytes try a sample pack containing small amounts of a variety of teas. This can be a wonderful, inexpensive way to taste several teas and find the ones you like without spending too much money.

Don't Go Cheap

If you're just getting started as a tea drinker, I recommend that you begin by buying medium- to medium-high-priced teas. Don't go cheap, but don't mortgage the house until you find the teas you know you like.

Storage

If possible, buy your tea in tins and transfer paper-wrapped tea to tins or ceramic jars. Air, moisture, and light are all enemies of stored tea. And a tin or jar kept very full means the tea will always be at its best.

Was It a Japanese Tea

or a Chinese Tea?

In finding your way through the world of tea, you may soon recognize the general types of green tea you prefer. If they are Japanese teas, remember that many Japanese teas employ the word *cha* in their name, as in Hojicha, Sencha, and so on. Chinese teas often employ words ending in a vowel followed by the letters *ng,* for example, *ong, ing, ung, eng.*

Web Sites

More and more mail-order houses are joining the cyber revolution and creating beautiful, user-friendly Web sites where you can not only purchase your tea, but also learn a great deal about current trends in the tea world. This is an explosive field, with new sites appearing all the time.

My Personal Favorites

When in doubt, I order from the Imperial Tea Court or Harney or Upton (see listings in the "Mail-Order Houses"). These are large, trustworthy houses, and I'm comfortable doing business with them. That said, I am not touting them as the only good ones. Finding great green tea is always an adventure. I never know where the next prize will come from. The market for green tea is so explosive and changeable right now, I urge you to try teas from a wide variety of houses. Some of the new small houses are just spectacular.

ABC TEA
Thomas Shu
14520 Arrow Highway
Baldwin Park, CA 91706
Phone: (626) 813-1333
abc_tea_house.htm

CHADO
Rheena Shah
8422½ West Third Street
Los Angeles, CA 90048
Phone: (800) 442-4019

FREED, TELLER & FREED
Karen Techeira
390 Swift Avenue #4
San Francisco, CA 94080
Phone: (650) 589-8500

HARNEY AND SONS
Village Green
P.O. Box 638
Salisbury, CT 06068
Phone: (800) TEA TIME
harney.com

IMPERIAL TEA COURT
1411 Powell Street
San Francisco, CA 94133
Phone: (415) 788-6080; Fax:
(415) 788-6079
imperialtea.com

MEM IMPORTS
Mark E. Mooradian
20 Flanders Road
Belmont, MA 02478
Phone: (800) 466-9399
memoorad@yahoo.com

RISHI TEA
Joshua Kaiser
207 East Buffalo Street
Milwaukee, WI 53202
rishi-tea.com

SILK ROAD TEAS
P.O. Box 287
Lagunitas, CA 94938
Phone: (415) 488-9017
tea-n-crumpets.com

TEAHOUSE KUAN YIN
1911 North 45th Street
Seattle, WA 98103
Phone: (206) 632-2055
teahousechoice.com

UPTON TEA IMPORTS
P.O. Box 159
Upton, MA 01568
Phone: (800) 234-8327

MARK T. WENDELL
P.O. Box 1312
West Concord, MA 01742
Phone: (508) 369-3709
marktwendell.com

INDEX

Tea is contentment . . . drinking tea,
desires diminish and I come to see the ancient
secret of happiness: wanting what I already have,
inhabiting the life that is already mine.

ANONYMOUS